Let's Explore
Neptune

Helen and David Orme

GARETH**STEVENS**
GS
PUBLISHING
A Member of the WRC Media Family of Companies

Please visit our web site at: www.garethstevens.com
For a free color catalog describing Gareth Stevens Publishing's list
of high-quality books and multimedia programs, call
1-800-542-2595 (USA) or 1-800-387-3178 (Canada).
Gareth Stevens Publishing's fax: (414) 332-3567.

Library of Congress Cataloging-in-Publication Data

Orme, Helen.
Let's explore Neptune / Helen and David Orme. — North American ed.
    p. cm. — (Space launch!)
Includes index.
ISBN-13: 978-0-8368-7944-5 (lib. bdg.)
ISBN-13: 978-0-8368-8129-5 (softcover)
    1. Neptune (Planet)—Juvenile literature. 2. Neptune (Planet)—Exploration—
Juvenile literature. I. Orme, David, 1948 Mar. 1- II. Title.
QB691.O76   2007
523.48'1—dc22   2006034805

This North American edition first published in 2007 by
Gareth Stevens Publishing
A Member of the WRC Media Family of Companies
330 West Olive Street, Suite 100
Milwaukee, Wisconsin 53212 USA

This U.S. edition copyright © 2007 by Gareth Stevens, Inc. Original edition copyright © 2006 by ticktock Entertainment
Ltd. First published in Great Britain in 2006 by ticktock Media Ltd., Unit 2, Orchard Business Centre, North Farm Road,
Tunbridge Wells, Kent, TN2 3XF, United Kingdom.

The publishers would like to thank: Sandra Voss, Tim Bones, James Powell, Indexing Specialists (UK) Ltd.

ticktock project editor: Julia Adams
ticktock project designer: Emma Randall

Gareth Stevens Editorial Direction: Mark Sachner
Gareth Stevens Editors: Barbara Kiely Miller and Carol Ryback
Gareth Stevens Art Direction: Tammy West
Gareth Stevens Designer: Dave Kowalski

Photo credits (t=top, b=bottom, c=center, l=left, r=right, bg=background)
Sam Chavan: 15tr; NASA: front cover, 1, 6tr, 7t, 8, 9cr, 11tl, 11tr, 15bl, 17tl, 18, 19, 20bl, 20cr, 22, 23; Science Photo Library: 4–5bg (original),
13, 14, 21; Shutterstock: 3bg, 6tl, 9bl, 17br; ticktock picture archive: 5, 6–7bg, 6bl, 7b, 9t, 10–11bg, 10, 11b, 12, 14–15bg, 16, 18–19bg, 22–23bg;
Rocket drawing Dave Kowalski/© Gareth Stevens, Inc.

Every effort has been made to trace the copyright holders for the photos used in this book. The publisher apologizes,
in advance, for any unintentional omissions and would be pleased to insert the appropriate acknowledgements in
any subsequent edition of this publication.

Printed in Canada

1 2 3 4 5 6 7 8 9 10 10 09 08 07 06

Contents

Words in the glossary are printed in **bold** the first time they appear in the text.

Where Is Neptune?

There are eight known planets in our **solar system**. The planets travel around the Sun. Neptune is the furthest planet from the Sun.

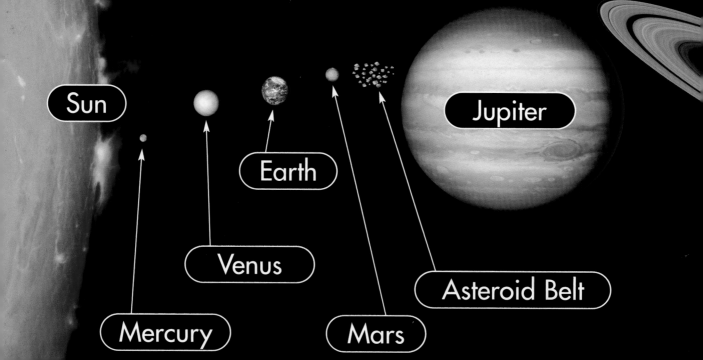

Sun

Mercury

Venus

Earth

Mars

Asteroid Belt

Jupiter

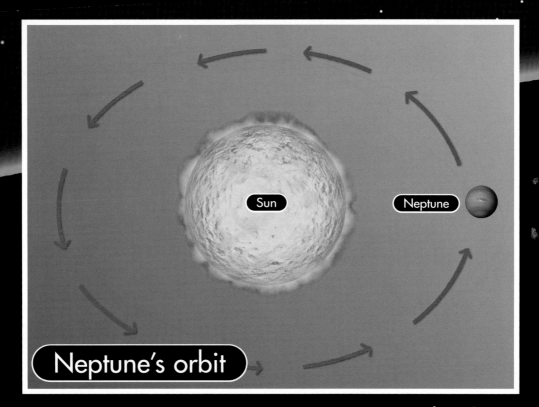

Neptune's orbit

The time a planet takes to travel around the Sun once is called a **year**. Neptune travels around the Sun once every 165 **Earth years**. This journey is called Neptune's **orbit**.

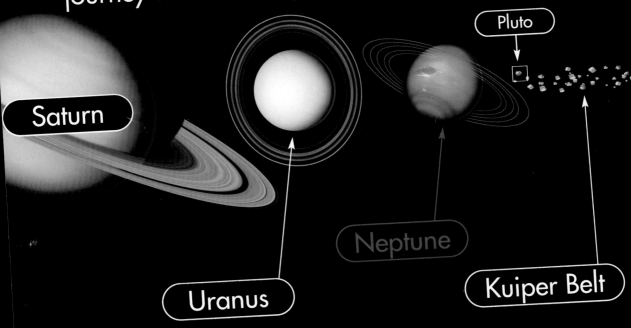

Saturn

Uranus

Neptune

Pluto

Kuiper Belt

Planet Facts

Neptune is the fourth biggest planet in the solar system. About 60 Earths could fit inside Neptune!

7,926 miles
(12,753 kilometers)

Earth

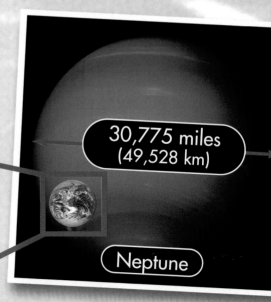

30,775 miles
(49,528 km)

Neptune

inside Neptune

Neptune has an **atmosphere** of gases. Beneath the atmosphere is a mixture of water, ices, and gases. The center, or core, of Neptune might be made of rock and ice.

Planets are always spinning. The time a planet takes to spin around once is called a **day**. One day on Neptune is the same as 16 hours on Earth.

direction of spin

Sometimes Neptune is farther away from the Sun than the **dwarf planet** Pluto. This happens when Pluto's orbit brings it closer to the Sun than Neptune.

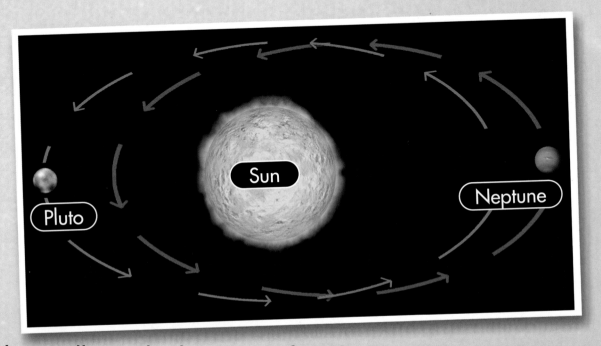

Sun

Pluto

Neptune

Pluto will not do this again for about another 230 years!

What's the Weather Like?

The fastest winds in the solar system roar around Neptune at speeds up to 1,300 miles (2,090 km) an hour! The fastest winds recorded on Earth were 231 miles (372 km) an hour.

These photographs of Neptune show clouds and bands of wind. They were taken by telescopes on Earth and by the **Hubble Space Telescope**.

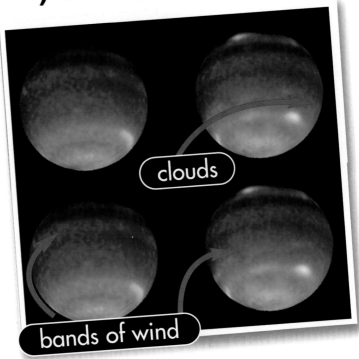

clouds

bands of wind

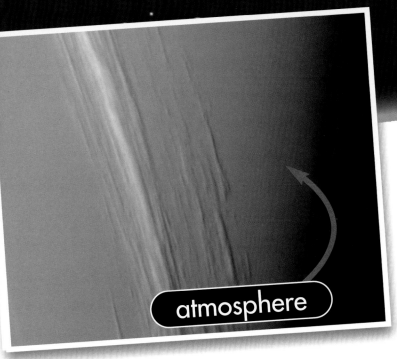

atmosphere

Neptune looks blue because the **methane gas** in its atmosphere absorbs all kinds of light but blue light.

Great Dark Spot

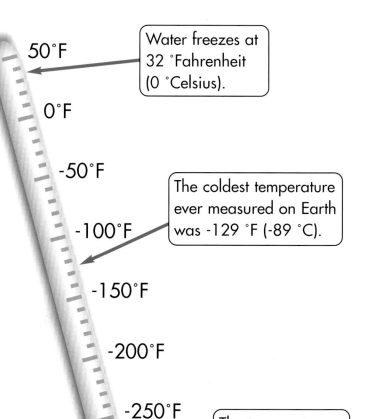

50°F

Water freezes at 32 °Fahrenheit (0 °Celsius).

0°F

-50°F

The coldest temperature ever measured on Earth was -129 °F (-89 °C).

-100°F

-150°F

-200°F

-250°F

The temperature of Neptune's atmosphere is -320 °F (-196 °C).

-300°F

This mark on Neptune is the Great Dark Spot, a storm as big as Earth! This photograph was taken by the *Voyager 2* **space probe** in 1989.

9

neptune's Moons

Astronomers have discovered 13 moons around Neptune. Earth has only one moon! The painting on this page shows three small moons that were discovered in 2002 and 2003.

Neptune

**2,160 miles
(3,475 km)**

Earth's Moon

Neptune's biggest moon is called Triton. It is about three-quarters the size of Earth's Moon.

**1,683 miles
(2,706 km)**

Triton

Neptune's moon Nereid has a very oval orbit. At its closest, Nereid is 507,500 miles (815,568 km) from Neptune. At its farthest, it is nearly 6 million miles (9.6 million km) from the planet!

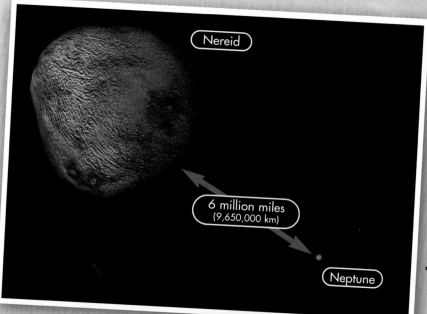

Nereid

6 million miles
(9,650,000 km)

Neptune

Triton

Triton is the coldest place in the solar system. The temperature on this moon is about -400 °F (-240 °C).

Scientists think that Triton did not form at the same time as Neptune.

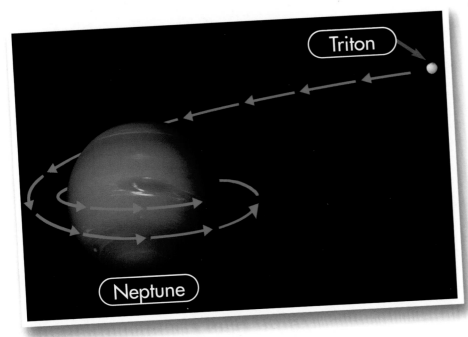

Triton

Neptune

Triton was probably moving through space when Neptune pulled this moon into orbit around it.

Triton is slowly getting closer to Neptune. It will probably crash into the planet in about 3 billion years.

Triton has **geysers**. They shoot icy gases and dust into the air. This material freezes and falls back down onto Triton like snow.

gases from a geyser being blown by strong winds

Neptune

a painting of Triton

Voyager 2 spotted one geyser shooting gases and ice 5 miles (8 km) high!

Neptune's Rings

Neptune has five complete rings. The rings are probably made of rocks and dust.

Neptune's neighbors Uranus and Saturn have rings, too. When their rings were discovered, astronomers guessed that Neptune might also have rings.

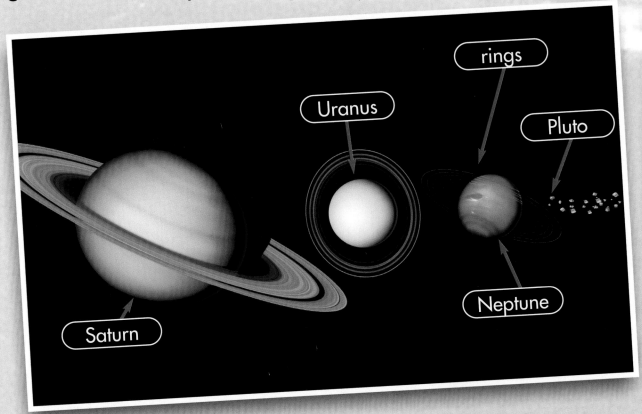

rings

Uranus

Pluto

Saturn

Neptune

But no one knew for sure until the space probe *Voyager 2* discovered Neptune's rings in 1989.

Scientists think that when rocks hit Neptune's moons, dust and bits of rock fly off into space. The dust and rocks are added to the planet's rings.

a painting of Neptune's rings

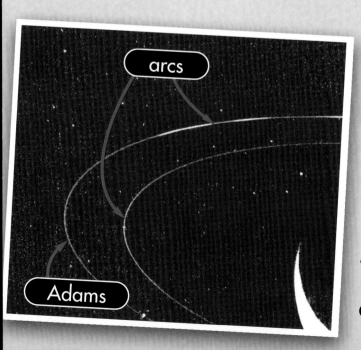

arcs

Adams

This photograph from *Voyager 2* shows the outer ring. It is called Adams.

The ring is thicker in some places than others. The thicker places are called arcs.

15

Neptune in History

Neptune was first identified by German astronomer Johann Galle in 1846.

Johann Galle

Before Galle discovered Neptune, its position in space had already been figured out. French scientist Urbain Joseph Le Verrier and English astronomer John Adams used mathematics to guess where Neptune was.

Neptune

In 1846, Johann Galle watched the sky where Le Verrier thought Neptune would be, and he found the planet!

Because it looks blue, the new planet was named after Neptune, the ancient Roman god of the sea.

The moon Triton was named after Neptune's son.

a statue of Neptune

What Can We See?

It is impossible to see Neptune without using a telescope because it is so far from Earth.

The best pictures of Neptune come from the *Hubble Space Telescope*. This telescope orbits Earth out in space.

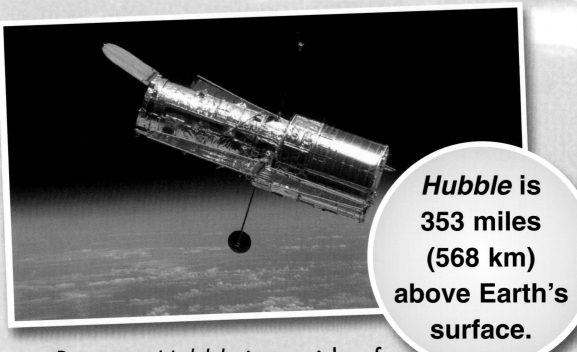

Hubble is 353 miles (568 km) above Earth's surface.

Because *Hubble* is outside of Earth's atmosphere, its pictures are much clearer than pictures from even the biggest telescopes on Earth.

These photos
taken by *Hubble* show spring on
the southern half of Neptune. They show the bands
of clouds in the south getting wider and brighter. This
is a sign of the Sun warming up this part of Neptune.

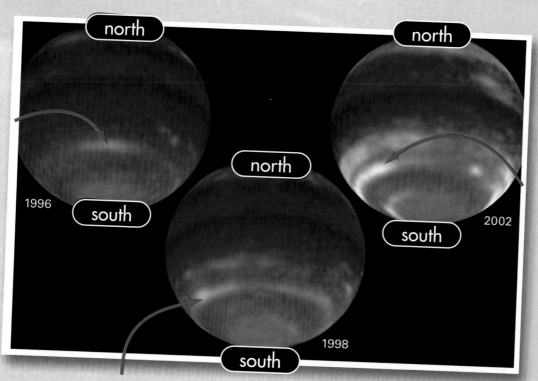

Because one year on Neptune lasts for 165 Earth years,
spring on Neptune lasts for about 40 Earth years!

Missions to Neptune

Voyager 2 is the only space mission that has been to Neptune. The *Voyager 2* space probe discovered Neptune's rings and some of its moons.

Voyager 2 blasted into space aboard a Titan-Centaur rocket on August 20, 1977.

Titan-Centaur rocket

Voyager 2

Voyager 2 traveled first to Jupiter, Saturn, and Uranus. It finally reached Neptune in 1989.

Voyager 2 measured
the temperatures on Neptune and
the wind speeds on the planet.

Voyager 2 is now
moving toward the
edge of our solar
system. Scientists
hope it will send
information back to
Earth until 2030.

Future Missions

NASA is planning a new mission to Neptune and its moons. If it goes ahead, the mission will be launched between 2016 and 2018. The spacecraft for this mission will arrive at Neptune in 2035!

Triton

The spacecraft will send two **landers** to Triton's surface.

In addition, space probes will be sent into Neptune's atmosphere.

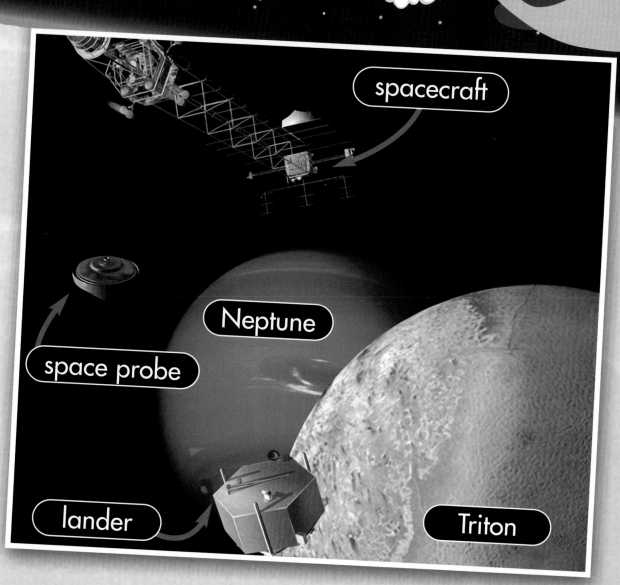

spacecraft

Neptune

space probe

lander

Triton

Neptune and Triton are very old. They have not
changed much since they were formed. Studying
them might give us new information about how our
solar system was formed.

Glossary

astronomers people who study outer space, often using telescopes

atmosphere the gases that surround a planet, moon, or star

day the time it takes a planet to spin around once. One day on Earth is twenty-four hours long.

dwarf planet a planet smaller than Mercury

Earth year the time it takes Earth to orbit the Sun once. An Earth year is 365 days long.

geysers a place on the surface of a planet or a moon where gases, ice, and water shoot into the air from time to time

Hubble Space Telescope a telescope that orbits Earth. Its pictures of space are very clear because it is outside of Earth's atmosphere.

landers spacecraft designed to land on a planet or moon.

methane gas a colorless gas that has no smell and burns easily

NASA (short for National Aeronautics and Space Administration) the U.S. space agency

orbit the path that a planet or other object takes when traveling around the Sun, or the path a satellite takes around a planet

solar system the Sun and everything that is in orbit around it

space probe a spacecraft sent from Earth to explore the solar system. It can collect samples and take pictures.

year the time it takes a planet to make a single orbit around the Sun

Index